thunderstorms

Alexis Evon

BookLeaf Publishing

India | USA | UK

Presentation by *BookLeaf Publishing*

Web: www.bookleafpub.com

E-mail: info@bookleafpub.com

ISBN: 9789360943578

First edition 2024

*dedicated to Alexis' eternal muse and forever
valentine, Nicolas*

ACKNOWLEDGEMENT

Alexis would like to thank their family and all of their chosen family, without whom this book wouldn't exist.

and Rachel. Fava Nava.

PREFACE

This is a collection of poems, caught like so
many thunderstorms in a jar.
Some are about grief, some about hope, all of
them about living. And
choosing to be Alive.

sensory overload

And just like THAT---
more like a clap than a snap---
the clouds began to pour.
With a beginning of whoosh
and a burst of thick drops
I heard it before
it began.
And smelled it,
Overwhelmingly.
My closed eyes,
face upturned,
see it best.
I stopped trying
for a taste long ago,
but will accept
a droplet
on my lips.
It feels like glitter
SHOULD feel.

mindful appreciation

Kurt Vonnegut advised us
to notice when we are happy
and comment
to ourselves

"If this isn't nice,
I don't know what is."

I recommend doing so aloud
so the people around
who hear you
can practice too

ghost light

bare stage
solitary light
(i like it best when it's green)

they say it is for the
spirits of the space
but it's also for the safety of the living.

the single bulb
on a simple stand
is replaced with gels and bogos
and bodies
telling stories.

laughter, tears, shock and awe
proceed to fill this echo chamber

and when it's done,
the bodies leave,
the laughter dies,
the ghost light returns---

center stage

to protect and comfort
any and all.

SO...

are there rules?
like, even guidelines?
    i'd sure love to have
    a quick notes guide
    on how to love.
well.
    not Love.
    like.
    how to like.

psh

    how to date.
yes?

at any rate,
    i'd buy the book

eerie

have you ever felt as though
you didn't exist?
like
you have the sudden need to scream
in someone's face
    "I'M HERE! LOOK AT ME!"

but that would be rude.
no.
the real reason
you don't do it
is because you are terrified
in the back of your mind
that they
    might not hear you...

that it's not all just an eerie feeling...

rather a fact of the world
and your "disappearing" act is successful.

or you were only ever a figment
of your own imagination.
    or someone else's

shadows

escaping from the world
traveling through this heaven
our hands and hearts betwirled
sitting beside my god among men
driving across states and lives
with snacks and smokes
and music and
love.

Someday we'll be happy and healthy
       calm and collected
       safe and sound.
i'll spend forever finding that with you.

  go back to sleep.
the world is too bitter
can't fulfill my desire
  go back and dream of yesterday
    that has slipped so far away
  and dream of tomorrow
    before it is here.

a little frantic

passionate.
that's the word I use
to describe myself
and my communication.

frantic
is also probably accurate.

the storm and fire
in my heart
and language
is quenched
by discomfort.

so if i am frantic
in your presence,
thank you for the safety.

luna

trust, but do not reach.
there are none to catch you–
we all are spiraling alone
through this cold empty tome.

the stars above are not
the hope that we imagined.
light in the endless dark;
more like a dead, distant spark.

more like the poison
which causes us to think
that we are anything more
than what we ever were before.

forever climbing,
never succeeding,
always trying,
wish for deleting,
not allowed to crack,
not allowed to crumble,
no wonder all my wishes
have always been so humble.

the Moon alone, she stands.

relentless, shifting, strong.
a reminder of what we all are;

Powerful but alone.

destruction prep

He said He was leaving
      He said He was leaving

and didn't know if He would be back.

He said He was leaving
      and I'm exploded
         imploded
         frozen
         on fire,
      drowned in emotion
         and tempest.

circles

i throw myself upon the shore
kicking
no longer screaming

i return

i angle myself hoping this time
will work.

i am disappointed

there is no hope
and i can't go on
my cries echoed
unheard
unanswered
unheeded

If we go
if this keeps happening
if reality doesn't sink in

we are taking you with us.

bravery

life is challenging
and being perceived
as a failure
is terrifying.

even---especially---
if we are just
a failure
to ourselves.

but to Try
knowing
that failure
could be imminent,
that fear
will be chasing,
that odds
are against
success.

but
to leap anyway?
to bare our souls everyday?
to Try, even after yesterday?

that is Courage.

bittersweet

I had a dream about You.
You came around a corner
and were suddenly THERE.

I crumpled to the ground
in disbelief and waterworks
and looked up at You in awe.

You are energy, a titan, a god.
I ran into Your arms,
and was unable to speak.

I tried to be selfless, to let You
connect with everyone else;
but I couldn't stop holding You.

I am trying to be strong,
to do all of the things that we love,
but this morning, I Miss You.

stubborn

I think my heart is just going to stop sometimes.
And yet it continues.

And my next breath feels like knives
as it runs through my lungs.

The horrors persist,
and so do i.

on an opening

my heart pounds upon my ribcage,
breaking my trepidatious hold
    on the leash of my nerves.

all of the lights and cues
all of the lines and props
all of the eyes
and minds
and
    hearts

the audience's first response;
primitive and honest
    intrigued or offended

the meaning sets in.
the point of the words, actions, jokes
the goal of the play
    in it's entirety.

a mind is engaged.
heart is not far behind.
    make them feel to help all heal.

serious messages are rarely fun

and always necessary.
how can we ever resolve
    if we only ignore?

self-inflicted

stress is a
    sinking feeling
my stomach falling
    into my knees
pressure abounds
    pushing and puking
too much strength
    of thoughts
too much strength
    of doubt
    of dread
    of hate
    of disappointment
knowing i will never
    achieve
what i set out to do

    my goal is void

music

music truly is

a release
a source of energy
a way to calm
a high
a life

for release
for romance
for friendship
for fantasy
for love

overwhelming
encouraging
Beautiful

thinking

i can't write in this state
my mind everywhere
thoughts pondering
it's not a headache---
    it's an escape attempt.

so many things to get out
and so many words
yet to be written
just precise thoughts
and too vague terms

language is so very
    versatile
but even this has no body
many ifs and ands and butts.
like the living languages
lack defined rules..

oh what a thing the
    human mind is.

unique

there's this thing inside me
that wants to be released
and i try to let it loose;
it refuses to be free.

i think i gotta push it
and force myself to fly
like a itty baby bird;
just commit to do or die.

there is no explanation
besides this feeling of more;
more excitement, more purpose,
more meaning, more lore.

it's a lot to ask,
but i can't help what I want.
should i forgo being me?
my own body just to haunt?

no. i won't.
for i am good.
people like me
are not understood

Frobard

its like lighting candles
trying to replace the sun

Thank you.
You're welcome.

I love you---always have.
I miss you---always will.

Flergin

a fae of a thing
feels almost unreal
certainly a changeling from birth.

barely "alive"
and yet so full of life
they are endlessly contradictory.

appreciated
loved and valued
but this doesn't change the feeling

of being wrong
in this world
in this time
in this life

maybe
someday
peace.

So We Will Wait.

thunderstorm person

first there came the rattle
The faintest hint of
      ROAR
like an angry whisper.
fury at indignities
      long past.
injustices ignored,
      seething.

then. the Rain.
an outpour, deluge
      waterfall of worthy affront.
a flash, illuminating all
with awesome lightning
      followed by a massive
CRACK
CLAP
      of thunder

The very earth shakes with it's rolling.